RADSPORTS GUIDES

SKATEBOARDING

TRACY NELSON MAURER

Rourke Publishing LLC
Vero Beach, Florida 32964

www.rourkepublishing.com

Project Assistance:
Ryan Leege from Freestyle of Duluth (F.O.D.), Duluth, MN, shared his expertise.

The author also extends appreciation to Mike Maurer, Kendall and Lois M. Nelson, Harlan Maurer, and Drs. Steven Massopust, Timothy Rich, and Boyd Erdman.

PHOTO CREDITS:
page 4 , 6, 17, 18, 28, 31, 32, 37, 39 ©East Coast Studios; pages 8, 23 ©Jaimie Squire; pages 10, 12, 21, 27, 29, 43 ©David Leeds/Allsport;

EDITORIAL SERVICES:
Pamela Schroeder

Notice: This book contains information that is true, complete, and accurate to the best of our knowledge. However, the author and Rourke Publishing LLC offer all recommendations and suggestions without any guarantees and disclaim all liability incurred in connection with the use of this information.

Safety first! Activities appearing or described in this publication may be dangerous. Always wear safety gear. Even with complete safety gear, risk of injury still exists.

Library of Congress Cataloging-in-Publication Data

Maurer, Tracy Nelson
   Skateboarding / Tracy Nelson Maurer
      p. cm — (Radsports guides)
      Includes bibliographical references and index.
      Summary: Surveys the history, equipment, techniques, and safety factors of skateboarding.
      ISBN 1-58952-104-8
         1. Skateboarding—Juvenile literature. [1. Skateboarding.] I. Title.

GV859.8 .M39 2001
796.22—dc21   2001041652

Printed in the U.S.A.

TABLE OF CONTENTS

Learning new tricks takes practice, dedication, and guts.

ART ON WHEELS

Skateboarders often feel strongly about their sport. Some skaters see skateboarding as an art form, like dance, music, or painting. They express themselves through flowing moves—spins, leaps, and slides—at breathtaking speed. Pavement becomes more than a stage: it works like a painter's canvas to add drama, depth, and style to the performance. Mostly, they just have fun.

chapter
ONE

INTENSE ACTION

Skateboarding gains some of its intense action from skaters just like you. Individuals, not teams, drive this sport. No coach runs you through drills or sets up your game plan. You do. You decide how far, how fast, and how big you want to go. Then you make it happen. It takes practice, **dedication,** and guts.

Even if you're a newbie, a beginner, you spend hours pushing the laws of physics to the brink. The basic principle of skateboarding pits speed and balance in a duel on top of a rather thin plank of wood. Your objectives include providing the energy to travel fast while you also provide the energy to keep upright on the board. Throw in a few tricks and watch Sir Isaac Newton and his physics buddies roll over in their graves.

SIMPLE WOODEN DEVICE

Skateboards started as simple wooden scooters with metal wheels in the early 1900s. They changed shapes over the years. Technology improved the design and parts. Manufacturers tried clay wheels in the 1960s, but settled on safer **urethane**, or heavy-duty plastic, in the 1970s. Urethane wheels cling to the surface, giving you traction.

Balancing on a speeding board looks easy, but it takes a lot of practice.

Graphic designs give skateboards a bit of attitude, but the images can wear off. Don't buy a board just for its looks.

BETTER DESIGNS

Over time, engineers tried many materials for the deck, or the main plank of the skateboard. Old-fashioned sugar maple wood proved the all-around winner for strength, flexibility, and control. Science made it better, though. Instead of a clunky hunk of wood, manufacturers usually use seven layers of **veneers**, or thin sheets of wood. Some use fewer layers; some use more.

Manufacturers glue the deck veneers together in special forms. The forms deliver about 300 psi (pounds per square inch) on the wood to set the glue and give the wood its concave, or curved, shape. A concave board's upturned nose, tail and edges deliver more control and strength.

The wood cures, or dries, for several days. Then special saws called routers hone the final shape before paint amps up the image. Graphic designs in cool patterns finish each board. Usually you see artwork, stickers, and logos under the board, since this area receives less thrashing than the topside. Even so, the graphics on the top and bottom wear off. Don't buy a board just for its looks.

RAD TIP

Under Pressure

How much pressure is 300 psi? Imagine two adults balancing on a single high heel of a woman's dress shoe. If they balanced on a sneaker, the pressure wouldn't be as great. (What hurts worse: when someone in high heels steps on your toes or someone in sneakers?) For a skateboard form, every square inch receives that same 300 psi pressure.

BUYING A BOARD

Since few places rent skateboards, you must borrow from friends or buy your own. You may want to buy your first board from a discount store or a toy store. Don't sneer. These assembled, ready-to-roll skateboards usually cost less than $50—a steal compared to serious boards. Discount brands may not last as long or perform as well as serious models, but they make great practice boards. You'll beat your board silly in the first few weeks.

DECK

WHEEL

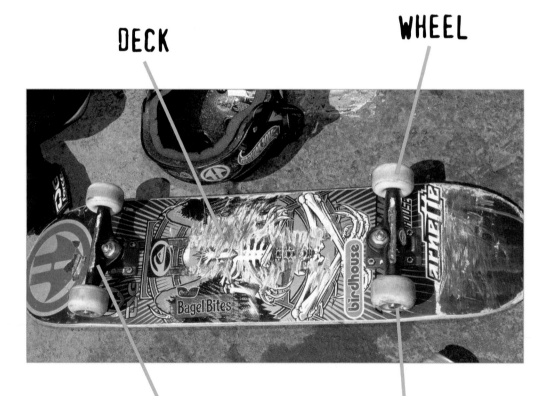

TRUCK

BEARINGS

You can always upgrade later. Check out the local skateboard or sport shops. Some surf, cycling, and ski shops also sell serious skateboarding equipment. You can find gear on the Internet, too. You buy the parts separately and assemble your ride.

Not counting tax and shipping, or any other funny fees, your board set-up will cost around $80 to $150. But don't blow your budget yet. You still need safety gear.

Deck — Most decks today are about 7 1/2" to 8" wide (19 to 20.3 cm) and 31" (78.74 cm) long, but shapes change over time. Avoid thick, hefty decks without concave shapes or your board won't pop, or lift, for tricks.

Trucks — Each truck, one front and one rear, contains an axle to hold the wheels. Look for lightweight and sturdy trucks that fit your riding style and skill level.

Wheels — Different wheels work better for certain skating styles. Wheels measure from about 40 to 88 millimeters. **Durometer** (duh ROM ih tur), the hardness, ranges from 60 to 101. Bigger, harder wheels build speed quickly but ride rough. Smaller, lighter wheels trade speed for board control. Softer wheels also add traction and a smoother ride. For starters, try 55 mm plain white wheels with a durometer of 99 or so. Then experiment.

Bearings — Bearings let the wheels spin freely. Look for smooth rolling bearings with easy-to-clean designs.

Grip tape — Grip tape keeps your feet from slipping. Stick it on the deck's topside.

Most skate parks and competitions require a helmet
and padding. Wear your armor every day.

PROTECT YOURSELF

Protect yourself with safety gear. You lose a lot of skating time if you crack your skull and mess up your brain.

Wear a helmet with the chin strap on. Brain buckets should fit snugly and not too tight. When you crash, the hard, plastic shell absorbs some of the impact. Foam padding inside the helmet softens the blow and cushions your noggin. Ride with your brain bucket on from the start. Then keep wearing it every day. Better riders fall less often, but they fall harder.

MORE ARMOR

Wrist guards brace your joints from twisting backwards. Since humans naturally try to break their falls by sticking out their hands, wrist guards prevent a lot of injuries.

You'll also need knee and elbow pads. This cushioned gear covers the two points on your body that tend to stick out most often. Hard plastic shells on the pads skid across the cement instead of your skin. Foam cushioning inside reduces the jolts to your joints. Straps hold them in place.

RAD TIP

Skin & Bones
If you're skinny, you may need to try Tony Hawk's idea for padding. He wore elbow pads on his knees.

13

YOU'RE NAKED UNDER THOSE CLOTHES

Cover up as much skin as you can, so you leave less on the pavement when you fall. Some serious riders even use gloves. Wear long sleeves and pants that give you room to move without too much geek factor.

Slip-resistant shoes also make sense. Your shoes form your braking system and wear out quickly from dragging on the pavement. Skate shoes handle the abuse and work better than normal street shoes.

READY TO ROLL

Before you dance with your skateboard, you need to know which foot leads. When you slide across your floor in stocking feet, which foot moves ahead? Many people lead with their left feet. Skaters call that a "regular-footed" stance. You're "goofy-footed" if you lead with the right. Riding goofy isn't bad or wrong, just different.

chapter
TWO

Your toes hang slightly over the edge. A sideways stance lets you **maneuver** the board by pressing the edges with your toes or your heels. Bend your knees and relax. Your arms and hands should stay about waist high. Keep them out where you can see them. If you snowboard or surf, the stance looks and feels very much the same. In the 1960s, the media called the sport "sidewalk surfing." Clever, huh?

HOP ON, NEWBIE

Find an open area with a flat, smooth surface for learning the basics. Try to avoid traffic and swarms of other skaters, walkers, or other dangerous **obstacles**.

Try these five steps to start rolling. Practice until riding feels comfortable.

1. Keep your back foot on the ground.
2. Place your lead foot on the deck near the front wheels.
3. Push off slowly with your back foot.
4. Bring your back foot up and place it near the tail.
5. Coast and hop off.

A mongo-footed rider puts the back foot on the deck and pushes off with the front foot. It still works, but a mongo start will slow your tricks. Style? Forget it.

TAKE A TURN

Turning comes next. Hop on and roll slowly across the flat surface. Lean slightly backward on your heels. You start turning, or carving, in that direction. Then lean slightly forward on your toes. You carve an arc in that direction. Practice turns over and over again.

Find an open area with a flat, smooth surface when you're first learning to ride.

A sliding stop takes practice. Don't try to skate in traffic until you can stop safely.

Learn to stop before you head out among other faster and bigger vehicles. Crashing works as a stopping maneuver, but it hurts. Jumping off also works, but it looks dweeby and lacks style.

Try a sliding stop. With your front foot still controlling the board, drop your back foot onto the ground. Let it slide along. Add pressure to come to a complete stop. For downhill stops, balance your weight on your front foot and use your back foot to stab at the pavement several times. You won't stop instantly but you stay in control of the board as you slow down. Most importantly, have fun.

AVOID PAIN

Skateboarders take risks every time they roll. You take home scabs, bumps, and bruises for prizes. Today's decks and wheels don't help any. Board designers traded stability for more speed and control. Still, skateboarding produces fewer doctor visits than soccer.

Almost a third of reported skateboard injuries occurs among riders with less than a week's worth of experience. From age ten through the teens, kids suffer mainly wrist and forearm sprains, strains, and fractures. They break their falls with their hands. Older kids still fall on their heads, but less often and much harder than little ankle-biters do. Avoid pain. Wear your helmet, wrist guards, and pads.

USE YOUR BRAIN

In addition to wearing protective gear, riding with your brain turned on also skips trips to the emergency center. Safety starts before you go. Check your board every time you ride. Fix or replace loose or broken parts, slippery top surfaces, and cracked wheels. Tighten your trucks.

Dial in your turns and stopping skills so you can handle hills. Ride ready to dodge vehicles, skaters, bicyclists, dogs, toddlers, walkers, joggers, and other surprises. Keep your speed in line with your skills.

Always scan the pavement ahead of you. Small, stiff skate wheels don't roll smoothly over sticks, stones, or holes in the pavement. Hitting these hazards causes instant wipe outs. You can't see these monsters in the dark, so don't ride at night.

EXACTLY HOW STUPID IS STUPID?

A few skateboarders give "stupid" new meaning. They skate in crowds of nonskaters. Sometimes they come in pairs, doubled up on one board. (One board, one person—it's very simple.)

The dumbest move of all is "truck-surfing" or "skitching" where a skater hangs onto a moving vehicle. Skaters can't match vehicle speed, cornering, and braking power. They crash into the vehicle, launch into traffic or face-plant on the asphalt.

RULES OF THE ROAD

Most falls happen in the road. Avoid skating on heavily traveled streets and watch every **intersection** carefully. Because you ride on wheels, you must obey traffic laws just like other vehicles.

1. Obey traffic laws.
2. Stay on the right side of a lane. Skate with traffic, never against it.
3. Give pedestrians the right of way. Always!

Ouch! Crashes happen. Crouch as you fall to soften the impact.

FALL RIGHT

You will fall. If you don't, you're not trying hard enough. Just fall the right way and get over it. Practice on grass or carpet first.

Crouching as you start to fall reduces the impact. Imagine throwing a wooden box out a third-story window. It crashes into tiny splinters upon impact. Throw the same box from a mailbox and it plops down with little damage. You work the same way. The higher you stand, the greater the impact when you fall.

Stay relaxed. A stiff body is like the wooden box—easy to splinter. Tuck your hands by your face or head; don't stick them out to stop yourself. Land on fleshy body parts, such as shoulders and hips. Roll when you drop so the impact moves across your entire body. Then stand up and try it again. Stop when you're tired or in pain.

SKID MARKS

Posers, those riders pretending to skateboard just to act cool, usually avoid road rash. They don't skate enough to collect real skid marks. Even with all the proper armor, you will leave patches of your skin on pavement somewhere.

Road rash looks nasty and stings. Wash it gently, put on **antiseptic** cream or spray, and let it heal without a bandage. You should check with a doctor if:

1. You spike a fever.
2. Red streaks show up around the wound.
3. Yellow pus oozes from it.
4. Dirt, gravel or glass won't wash out.
5. You can see lots of meaty flesh or white bone.

Don't mess around. Infections can keep you off your board for weeks. Compound fractures, or broken bones poking through the skin, need medical attention. Don't move the part that's broken (you won't want to anyway). You can expect at least three months to heal from those doozies.

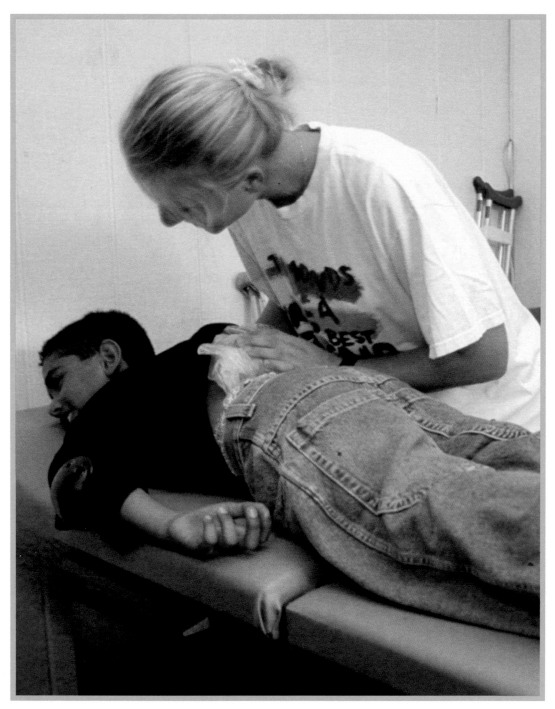

Put safety first when you skate and avoid those pesky emergency room visits.

Sprains from twisting **ligaments** swell up the joint areas, such as ankles, wrists, or fingers. Strains usually swell less than sprains but bruise more often, since they come from twisting the muscles the wrong way. A bad sprain or strain can take you off your board for up to four weeks.

Also, you may see stars after a severe head-banging or, for the boys, rackings from unnaturally straddling a hand rail. Sit down with your head between your knees. If your vision stays cloudy or if you feel stabbing pains anywhere, ask someone to bring you to the doctor right away.

Skate safely and you skate longer. Anything less isn't much fun.

RAD TIP

Road rash can gross out your parents and dating partners. Cover skid wounds with gauze for public appearances. As it heals, the scab may feel tight and break when you ride. Try a thin layer of petroleum jelly to soften it.

SKATEBOARDING'S RALLY

Since skateboarding began in the 1960s, the sport has rolled in and out of popularity several times. It seems to rally about every ten years, gathering new riders and fans each time. The favored skating styles change with each comeback, too.

In the 1970s, skaters competed mainly for speed. Ten years later, freestyle contests with precise flatland routines set to music became popular. Next, freestyle tricks in bowls, or sunken ramps shaped like empty swimming pools, drew riders and gawkers. Vert, or half-pipes with vertical walls, also created a huge following. Then the sport faded, waiting for the next big thing.

chapter

THREE

STREET SKATING ARRIVES

Insurance pressures closed most skate parks by the 1990s. It cost too much to keep the parks open. Riders took to the streets. Then the sport's first long-lasting rally began. ESPN's X Games helped, too.

Street skating combines the technical moves of flatland freestyle and the **amplitude**, or height, of vert. You need sharp skills to explore the urban terrain. Jumping huge gaps, grinding hand rails, and bumping down stairs takes practice.

RIDE ON THE RIGHT SIDE OF THE LAW

Know where you can ride legally. Ask permission. Call your local police station. Many cities banned skateboards from public areas in the 1970s. Police still give tickets. Fines add up quickly.

Some rough and reckless street riders hyped the rebel side of the sport. They took an "us-against-them" attitude and showed a dark side of skateboarding. Ignore it.

Help city officials ditch the old bans by setting a good example. Work with schools and local leaders to teach the community about skateboarding. You might even gain support for a skate park to keep kids off the street.

The law is on your side now. The International Association of Skateboard Companies (IASC) has worked to make skateboarding an official "**hazardous** activity." By law, participants in hazardous activities take responsibility for their actions and cannot sue if injured at a public facility. City skate parks can open again without fear of huge lawsuits.

Choose your skate location wisely. Many people do not allow skaterboarders near their homes and businesses because of the damage they can cause.

Most kids master the basic moves in their driveways.

WHERE TO SKATE

Thanks to the ups and downs of the sport, you can find more places to skate and try more styles of skating today than any other time in skateboarding's history.

Most skaters start in their driveways. The flat surface works well for building basic skills and for simple flatland tricks. You can build small wooden ramps for your home, too. Check out the skateboarding magazines or websites for plans. If you design your own, include plenty of bracing. Falling through the ramp deck ruins even simple tricks.

Before you start construction, ask permission. Promise to bring back any tools that you borrow. Scam scrap wood, with permission, if you can't afford to buy new. Soon you'll have your own private launch pad.

AMPED RAMPS AT THE PARK

Start asking around your school and at the local skate shop for places to skate. You might have a skate park within driving distance. Before you jump in anywhere, scope it out. Watch the order of the skaters. See who skates first and how they handle snaking, or cutting in front of other riders.

Skate parks feature specially designed courses and ramps where riders can focus on tricks instead of watching for cars. A few companies specialize in creating these parks, using professional surfaces and proven safety techniques. Some skate parks charge admission fees. Some are free. Either way, a well-built park delivers endless opportunities for radical fun.

Dropping in looks easy, but it takes practice. Keep your knees bent and loose for better control.

29

BRAVE THE VERT

Today's skate parks usually include 3 foot (.9 m) to 6 foot (1.8 m) mini-ramps. Some have half-pipes with vertical walls to launch you straight up into the air. All vert ramps look much higher when you're standing on the deck looking down. Some look downright scary.

One way to brave the vert is the bottom-up technique. Start carving the pipe from the bottom floor, making huge arcs across the tranny, the curved sections between the flat floor and vertical walls. Once you feel comfortable with that, start pumping or bending your knees and arms until you build enough **momentum** to ride all the way up to the deck and back down again.

You can also practice on a parking curb or a mini-ramp at home. With your back foot on the tail to hold the board, lock your rear wheels against the coping. Stick the board out over the edge. Step on with your front foot. Lean over and bring up your back foot, keeping your knees bent and loose. When all four wheels make contact with the wall, center your weight. This beats a ride at the fair, guaranteed.

The back foot holds the board steady. Step on with the front foot and lean forward. Lift off the back foot and center your weight.

Longboards deliver a smooth, fast ride.

MORE WAYS TO WHEEL

Explore all of the basic skateboarding styles—freestyle, vert, jumps and street—when you feel ready. Don't push too far too fast. Skills come with time and practice.

You might find that you crave more speed than your 31" (78.7 cm) board can deliver. Longboards, originally knock offs of surfboards, now attract downhill racers and geezer cruisers. They range in length from 38" to 60" (96.5 to 152.4 cm) and ride on softer, larger wheels. They carve like a hot knife in butter, and they glide right over sidewalk cracks. Riders with knee trouble like the longboards for the smooth ride. Surfers and snowboarders use them for cross-training. The trick riders started messing with them, too; it probably won't be long before you see these boards everywhere.

You may also see more stand-up racing. Riders surf downhill courses at speeds regularly topping 45 mph (72 kph) and reaching as high as 61 mph (97.6 kph). Similarly, the street luge pushes speeds of 70 mph (112 kph). Riders lie down on modified boards to charge down steep courses. Stand-up racing and street luge require precise skills and extra safety measures, including full-face helmets.

BOARD CARE

Skateboards last longer with a little care. Protect your bearings by avoiding puddles and other water spots. Extreme drenching and direct sun or heat may affect the wood in your board. Store it indoors.

Make a **maintenance** checklist and post it in your garage. Date it every time you work on your board. You may need to buy a few tools before you start. Your local skate shop can help you out.

BEARINGS
Care Time: 20 minutes
Tools: Paint thinner, paper towels, bearing lubricant
(optional—ask at your skate shop)

Remove the wheel by unscrewing the axle nut. Dab your paper towel in the paint thinner and wipe the outside of the bearing. Place the paper towel over the axle and press the wheel onto it. Spin the wheel to clean the inside. Turn it over and repeat. Replace the wheel, but don't put the nut on. Add a drop of lubricant to each side. Spin the wheel several times. Then replace the axle nut. Repeat the entire process for each wheel.

TRUCKS
Care Time: 5 minutes
Tools: Screwdriver

Test the hardware on each truck. If the trucks are loose, you'll ride on wobbly wheels (but probably not too far). Tighten any loose trucks.

DECK
Care Time: 10 minutes (plus drying time for the glue)
Tools: Carpenter's wood glue and vice or clamp

Check your deck for cracks and chips. You can repair some dingers if the chip is still attached. Squeeze a bit of carpenter's wood glue into the divot and clamp the chip into place. Did you find large cracks or missing chunks? Replace your board.

WHEELS
Care Time: 5 minutes
Tools: Screwdriver

Check your wheels for large nicks and cracks. Replace worn wheels by removing the axle nut. Slip the old wheel off. Put the new wheel on. Tighten the axle nut. Some people replace all four wheels at once. Others replace as needed. Do whatever works for you.

TRICKS AGAIN AND AGAIN

Skateboarders started their own party on wheels. Join in when you're ready. Tricks take time to master. Think of those duffers on the golf courses. They play day after day, trying for **consistent** moves and better scores. Nobody cheers them on. They play only for their personal best. They play because they love to play. That's the soul of skateboarding, too.

Consistency counts. Some skaters can nail a risky trick once in a while. Whether you strive for technical stunts or bust-out air, you need to control the moves over and over again.

chapter

FOUR

POP OFF

Skateboarding covers more than 40 years. Every year, new tricks appear and the sport continues to grow. What's sick, or cool, today could be dull tomorrow. Check the skate park, the skating magazines, and the Internet for the latest trick tips. Watch skateboarding videos to study the moves frame by frame.

A few tricks seem to hold steady over time. Start with these basics before you move onto airs (aerial tricks):

BASIC
1. Ollie

Rolling across a flat surface at a medium speed, move your front foot to the middle of the board. Place the ball of your back foot mid-tail. Bend your knees and slam down on the tail by boning (straightening) your back leg. This unweights the front and pops the board off the ground. Level out the board by rolling your front foot sideways, sliding up the grip tape, and pushing on the nose. Pull your back leg up toward your chest. Keep your knees bent as you land to absorb the impact. Practice and increase your speed. You pop up higher and fly farther as you go faster.

Pull your knees up toward your chest on an ollie to gain more air.

2. Manual

"Old School" or pre-1990s riders call this a Wheelie. While riding at a medium speed, press your weight on your back foot at the tail until the front truck pops up. Balance with your arms and keep the tail from kissing the cement. Drop your weight forward to bring the nose back down. A Nose Manual uses the same moves in reverse. Your weight pushes the nose down and your rear truck pops up.

3. Ollie To Manual

Skateboarding becomes more and more difficult as you combine tricks and create a steady flow of moves. For this combination, you ollie onto a long concrete ledge but land on your back two wheels. Balance and hold the manual steady. Then land the front wheels and ride off. Kickflip to manuals and other footwork tricks follow this one.

INTERMEDIATE

1. Grinds

When you feel steady on your board and you ollie easily, start grinding, or sliding on the axles. For a frontside 50-50 grind, ollie up to a curb or rail with your weight shifted slightly forward to land the trucks straight. Bend your knees and use your arms for balance. As you reach the end of the grinding surface, press your tail back to pop up a bit. This helps to keep you from slamming forward.

◀ *Riding switch-stance, or fakie, doubles your trick library. Here, the boy pulls a fakie off the ramp.*

▲

He's regular-footed, so he normally rides with his left foot forward. He comes off the ramp with his right foot ahead for a fakie.

◀ *Notice how his knees stay bent to cushion the impact.*

2. Switch-Stance

After you have a decent library of tricks, start pulling the same tricks from the reverse stance. Put your back foot forward and the front foot back. You double your bag of tricks.

ADVANCED

Experienced riders throw big-air stunts, including flips, spins, and handstands. How big is big air? Try 16 feet (4.9 m) above the coping—higher than a house. Oh, no—you won't find any tips for these radical moves here. If you're that good, you can ask the other pros how they do it.

THRASH IT OUT

When ESPN broke out with the X Games concept, skateboarders snapped to attention. Some thought it looked too slick and too **commercial**. Most watched it anyway. They tried to catch each event to see the newest tricks. Pro skaters realized that the X Games offered an opportunity to show their sport to the world. It worked.

chapter

A WORLD OF WHEELS

Men and women around the world push the sport to the edge, adding new moves and raising the standards. Huge skating showdowns like the B3 (bikes, blades and boards) event and the Vans Triple Crown series feature the biggest names in the sport. Tours and demos criss-cross the globe, highlighting slalom, park, best trick and vert events. For fans, seeing the skaters perform live brings a new excitement to the sport.

Name: Tony Hawk
Born: 5/12/68
Height: 6' 2" (1.8 m)
Weight: 170 lbs. (77.1 kg)
Hometown: San Diego, California
First contest: 11 years old

Tony Hawk, nicknamed "The Birdman," ranks as a skateboarding legend. During the first two decades that he skated, he created more than 80 tricks and landed the sport's first 900. He won twice as many professional contests as any other skater. Now Tony runs an equipment manufacturing company, performs in commercials and exhibitions, and saves time to do dad things with his two sons.

Tony Hawk flies through the air at the X Games in San Francisco, August 2000.

PRO SPOTLIGHT:
Name: Cara-Beth Burnside
Born: Leo
Height: 5' 3" (1.6 m)
Weight: 120 lbs. (54.4 kg)
Hometown: Orange, CA
Started skating: Age 11

Women's skateboarding found a leader in Cara-Beth Burnside. This agile and fierce skater won the Vans Triple Crown of Skateboarding Female Soul Bowl Contest and often rips right past the guys. Cara-Beth turned pro in 1990 and became the first female to get a shoe sponsorship, skating on the Vans team. In addition to hard-core skateboarding, Cara-Beth also ranks among the best snowboarders.

Europeans kept freestyle competitions running and developed a precise scoring system. The U.S. prefers "street" skating competitions with courses winding in, over, and through obstacles. These courses look nothing like the streets you find in the real world, but they're even more fearsome to ride.

Local skateboarding competitions pop up everywhere for **amateurs**. Check your favorite sport shop for contests near you. Pros also endorse local shops, the first step to sponsorship. The next big name in skateboarding could be yours!

FURTHER READING

Your library and the Internet can help you learn more about skateboarding. Check these titles and sites for starters:

Brooke, Michael. *The Concrete Wave: The History of Skateboarding*. Warwick Publishing, 1999.

Hawk, Tony and Sean Mortimer. *Hawk – Occupation: Skateboarder*. HarperColins Publishers, 2000.

Nabhan, Marty. *Pro-Am Sports: Skateboarding*. The Rourke Corporation, 1994.

WEBSITES TO VISIT

expn.go.com

www.heckler.com

www.monsterskate.com

www.exploratorium.edu/skateboarding

www.thrashermagazine.com

www.transworldmatrix.com

www.trueride.com

www.vans.com

www.wcs.wmc.org

www.withitgirl.com/sports

GLOSSARY

amateurs (AM uh churz) — athletes without professional skill; contests with no prize money

amplitude (AM pluh tood) — height, big air

antiseptic (an tih SEP tik) —a lotion, cream, or spray that kills germs

commercial (kah MUR shul) — for profit or money

consistent (kun SIS tent) — the same over and over again; not changing

dedication (ded ih KAY shun) — whole-hearted action; devotion or commitment

durometer (duh ROM ih tehr) — a device used to measure hardness; also, the measure of hardness

hazardous (HAZ urd us) — dangerous

intersection (in tur SEK shun) — where streets cross or meet

ligaments (LIG ah ments) — strong bands that tie bones together and steady the joints

maintenance (MAYN tuh nins) — care; cleaning and repairing to keep something working well

maneuver (mah NOO vur) — movement or action

momentum (mom MEN tum) — forward motion, movement

obstacles (OB stuh kilz) — things blocking a path, such as jumps, rails or gaps

urethane (YER uh thayn)— extra-strong plastic

veneers (vuh NEERZ)— thin sheets of wood

INDEX

ABOUT THE AUTHOR

Tracy Nelson Maurer specializes in nonfiction and business writing. Her most recently published children's books include the A to Z series, also from Rourke Publishing LLC. She lives with her husband Mike and two children in Superior, Wisconsin.